Dickinson on Love

Warbler Press

Emily Dickinson's poems were first published between 1890 and 1896 in three volumes, edited by Thomas Wentworth Higginson and Mabel Todd. Dickinson's niece Martha Dickinson Bianchi edited and published several subsequent collections including *The Single Hound* (1914) and *Complete Poems* (1924).

Biographical Note and About This Book © 2020 Ulrich Baer

ISBN 978-1-7345881-4-9 (paperback)
ISBN 978-1-7345881-5-6 (e-book)

warblerpress.com

Current and forthcoming titles in the
Warbler Press Contemplations series at
warblerpress.com

Publisher's note: This edition follows the punctuation, lineation, and spelling established in *The Poems of Emily Dickinson* edited by R. W. Franklin (Cambridge: The Belknap Press of Harvard University Press, 1999).

Dickinson on Love

Emily Dickinson

Edited by Ulrich Baer

CONTENTS

Dickinson on Love

That love is all there is
Is all we know of Love,
It is enough, the freight should be
Proportioned to the groove.

It's all I have to bring today -
This, and my heart beside -
This, and my heart, and all the fields -
And all the meadows wide -
Be sure you count - sh'd I forget
Some one the sum could tell -
This, and my heart, and all the Bees
Which in the Clover dwell.

Mine - by the Right of the White Election!
Mine - by the Royal Seal!
Mine - by the sign in the Scarlet prison -
Bars - cannot conceal!
Mine - here - in Vision - and in Veto!
Mine - by the Grave's Repeal -
Titled - Confirmed -
Delirious Charter!
Mine - long as Ages steal!

You left me- sire, two Legacies -
A Legacy of Love
A Heavenly Father would suffice
Had He the offer of -

You left me Boundaries of Pain -
Capacious as the Sea -
Between Eternity and Time -
Your Consciousness - and me -

Alter! When the Hills do -
Falter? When the Sun
Question if His Glory
Be the Perfect One -

Surfeit? When the Daffodil
Doth of the Dew -
Even as Herself - Sir -
I will- Of You -

Doubt Me! My Dim Companion!
Why, God, would be content
With but a fraction of the Life -
Poured thee, without a stint -
The whole of me - forever -
What more the Woman can,
Say quick, that I may dower thee
With last Delight I own!

It cannot be my spirit -
For that was thine, before -
I ceded all of Dust I knew -
What Opulence the more
Had I - a freckled Maiden,
Whose farthest of Degree,
Was - that she might -
Some distant Heaven,
Dwell timidly - with thee!

Sift her, from Brow to Barefoot!
Strain till your last Surmise -
Drop, like a Tapestry, away,
Before the Fire's Eyes -
Winnow her finest fondness -
But hallow just the snow
Intact, in Everlasting flake -
Oh, Caviler, for you!

If you were coming in the Fall,
I'd brush the Summer by
With half a smile, and half a spurn,
As Housewives do, a Fly.

If I could see you in a year,
I'd wind the months in balls -
And put them each in separate Drawers,
For fear the numbers fuse -

If only Centuries, delayed,
I'd count them on my Hand,
Subtracting, till my fingers dropped
Into Van Dieman's Land.

If certain, when this life was out -
That your's and mine, should be -
I'd toss it yonder, like a Rind,
And take Eternity -

But, now, uncertain of the length
Of this, that is between,
It goads me, like the Goblin Bee -
That will not state - it's sting.

I hide myself - within my flower,
That fading from your Vase -
You - unsuspecting - feel for me -
Almost - a loneliness -

That I did always love
I bring thee Proof
That till I loved
I never lived - Enough -

That I shall love alway -
I argue thee
That love is life -
And life hath Immortality -

This - dost thou doubt - Sweet -
Then have I
Nothing to show
But Calvary -

Have you got a Brook in your little heart,
Where bashful flowers blow,
And blushing birds go down to drink -
And shadows tremble so -

And nobody knows, so still it flows,
That any brook is there,
And yet your little draught of life
Is daily drunken there -

Why - look out for the little brook in March,
When the rivers overflow,
And the snows come hurrying from the hills,
And the bridges often go -

And later, in August it may be,
When the meadows parching lie,
Beware, lest this little brook of life,
Some burning noon go dry!

As if some little Arctic flower
Opon the polar hem -
Went wandering down the Latitudes
Until it puzzled came
To continents of summer -
To firmaments of sun -
To strange, bright crowds of flowers -
And birds, of foreign tongue!
I say, As if this little flower
To Eden, wandered in -
What then? Why nothing,
Only, your *inference* therefrom!

My River runs to Thee -
Blue Sea - Wilt welcome me?

My River waits reply.
Oh Sea - look graciously!

I'll fetch thee Brooks
From spotted nooks -

Say Sea - take me?

I cannot live with You -
It would be Life -
And Life is over there -
Behind the Shelf

The Sexton keeps the key to -
Putting up
Our Life - His Porcelain -
Like a Cup -

Discarded of the Housewife -
Quaint - or Broke -
A newer Sevres pleases -
Old Ones crack -

I could not die - with You -
For One must wait
To shut the Other's Gaze down -
You - could not -

And I - Could I stand by
And see You - freeze -
Without my Right of Frost -
Death's privilege?

Nor could I rise - with You -
Because Your Face
Would put out Jesus' -
That New Grace

Glow plain - and foreign
On my homesick eye -
Except that You than He
Shone closer by -

They'd judge Us - How -
For You - served Heaven - You know,
Or sought to -
I could not -

Because You saturated sight -
And I had no more eyes
For sordid excellence
As Paradise

And were You lost, I would be -
Though my name
Rang loudest
On the Heavenly fame -

And were You - saved -
And I - condemned to be
Where You were not
That self - were Hell to me -

So we must meet apart -
You there - I - here -
With just the Door ajar
That Oceans are - and Prayer -
And that White Sustenance -
Despair -

'Twas a long Parting - but the time
For Interview - had Come -
Before the Judgment Seat of God -
The last - and second time

These Fleshless Lovers met -
A Heaven in a Gaze -
A Heaven of Heavens - the Privilege
Of One another's Eyes -

No Lifetime set - on Them -
Appareled as the new
Unborn - except They had beheld -
Born infiniter - now -

Was Bridal - e'er like This?
A Paradise - the Host -
And Cherubim - and Seraphim -
The unobtrusive Guest -

There came a Day - at Summer's full -
Entirely for me -
I thought that such - were for the Saints -
Where Resurrections - be -

The Sun - as common - went abroad -
The Flowers - accustomed - blew -
As if no Soul the Solstice passed -
That maketh all things new.

The time was scarce profaned - by speech -
The symbol of a word
Was needless - as at Sacrament -
The Wardrobe - of Our Lord -

Each was to each - the sealed church -
Permitted to commune - this time -
Lest we too awkward - show -
At "Supper of the Lamb."

The hours slid fast - as hours will -
Clutched tight - by greedy hands -
So - faces on two Decks - look back -
Bound to opposing Lands -

And so - when all the time had failed -
Without external sound -
Each - bound the other's Crucifix -
We gave no other bond -

Sufficient troth - that we shall rise -
Deposed - at length - the Grave -
To *that* New Marriage -
Justified - through Calvaries of Love!

I'm ceded - I've stopped being Their's -
The name They dropped opon my face
With water, in the country church
Is finished using, now,
And They can put it with my Dolls,
My childhood, and the string of spools,
I've finished threading - too -

Baptized, before, without the choice,
But this time, consciously, Of Grace -
Unto supremest name -
Called to my Full - The Crescent dropped -
Existence's whole Arc, filled up,
With one - small Diadem -

My second Rank - too small the first -
Crowned - Crowing - on my Father's breast -
A half unconscious Queen -
But this time - Adequate - Erect,
With Will to choose,
Or to reject,
And I choose, just a Crown -

Elysium is as far as to
The very nearest Room
If in that Room a Friend await
Felicity or Doom -

What fortitude the Soul contains,
That it can so endure
The accent of a coming Foot -
The opening of a Door -

I'm "wife" - I've finished that -
That other state -
I'm Czar - I'm "Woman" now -
It's safer so -

How odd the Girl's life looks
Behind this soft Eclipse -
I think that Earth feels so
To folks in Heaven - now -

This being comfort - then
That other kind - was pain -
But Why compare?
I'm "Wife"! Stop there!

She rose to His Requirement - dropt
The Playthings of Her Life
To take the honorable Work
Of Woman, and of Wife -

If ought She missed in Her new Day,
Of Amplitude, or Awe -
Or first Prospective - or the Gold
In using, wear away,

It lay unmentioned - as the Sea
Develope Pearl, and Weed,
But only to Himself - be known
The Fathoms they abide -

Come slowly - Eden!
Lips unused to Thee -
Bashful - sip thy Jessamines -
As the fainting Bee -

Reaching late his flower,
Round her chamber hums -
Counts his nectars -
Enters - and is lost in Balms

Of all the Souls that stand create -
I have Elected - One -
When Sense from Spirit - files away -
And Subterfuge - is done -
When that which is - and that which was -
Apart - intrinsic - stand -
And this brief Drama in the flesh -
Is shifted - like a Sand -
When Figures show their royal Front -
And Mists - are carved away,
Behold the Atom - I preferred -
To all the lists of Clay!

I have no Life but this -
To lead it here -
Nor any Death - but lest
Dispelled from there -
Nor tie to Earths to come,
Nor Action new
Except through this Extent
The love of you.

Your Riches - taught me - Poverty.
Myself - a Millionaire
In little Wealths, as Girls could boast
Till broad as Buenos Ayre -

You drifted your Dominions -
A Different Peru -
And I esteemed all Poverty
For Life's Estate with you -

Of Mines, I little know, myself -
But just the names, of Gems -
The Colors of the Commonest -
And scarce of Diadems -

So much, that did I meet the Queen -
Her Glory I should know -
But this, must be a different Wealth -
To miss it - beggars so -

I'm sure 'tis India - all Day -
To those who look on You -
Without a stint - without a blame,
Might I - but be the Jew -

I'm sure it is Golconda -
Beyond my power to deem -
To have a smile for mine - each Day,
How better, than a Gem!

At least, it solaces to know
That there exists - a Gold -
Altho' I prove it, just in time
It's distance - to behold -

It's far - far Treasure to surmise -
And estimate the Pearl -
That slipped my simple fingers through -
While just a Girl at school.

I gave Myself to Him -
And took Himself, for Pay -
The solemn contract of a Life
Was ratified, this way -

The Wealth might disappoint -
Myself a poorer prove
Than this great Purchaser suspect,
The Daily Own - of Love

Depreciate the Vision -
But till the Merchant buy -
Still Fable - in the Isles of spice -
The subtle Cargoes - lie -

At least - 'tis Mutual - Risk -
Some - found it - Mutual Gain -
Sweet Debt of Life - Each Night to owe -
Insolvent - every Noon -.

Going to Him! Happy letter!
Tell Him -
Tell Him the page I did'nt write -
Tell Him - I only said the Syntax -
And left the Verb and the pronoun - out -
Tell Him just how the fingers hurried -
Then - how they waded - slow - slow -
And then you wished you had eyes in your pages -
So you could see what moved them so -

Tell Him - it was'nt a Practised Writer -
You guessed - from the way the sentence toiled -
You could hear the Boddice tug, behind you -
As if it held but the might of a child -
You almost pitied it - you - it worked so -
Tell Him - No - you may quibble there -
For it would split His Heart, to know it -
And then you and I, were silenter.

Tell Him - Night finished - before we finished -
And the Old Clock kept neighing "Day"!
And you - got sleepy -
And begged to be ended -
What would it hinder so - to - say?
Tell Him - just how she sealed you - Cautious!
But - if He ask where you are hid
Until tomorrow - Happy letter!
Gesture Coquette - and shake your Head!

The Way I read a Letter's - this -
'Tis first - I lock the Door -
And push it with my fingers - next -
For transport it be sure -

And then I go the furthest off
To counteract a knock -
Then draw my little Letter forth
And slowly pick the lock -

Then - glancing narrow, at the Wall -
And narrow at the floor
For firm Conviction of a Mouse
Not exorcised before -

Peruse how infinite I am
To no one that You - know -
And sigh for lack of Heaven - but not
The Heaven God bestow -.

Wild nights - Wild nights!
Were I with thee
Wild nights should be
Our luxury!

Futile - the winds -
To a Heart in port -
Done with the Compass -
Done with the Chart!

Rowing in Eden -
Ah - the Sea!
Might I but moor - tonight -
In thee!

"The Night was wide, and furnished scant
With but a single Star -
That often as a Cloud it met -
Blew out itself - for fear -

The Wind pursued the little Bush -
And drove away the Leaves
November left - then clambered up
And fretted in the Eaves -

No Squirrel went abroad -
A Dog's belated feet
Like intermittent Plush, be heard
Adown the empty street -

To feel if Blinds be fast -
And closer to the fire -
Her little Rocking Chair to draw -
And shiver for the Poor -

The Housewife's gentle Task -
How pleasanter - said she
Unto the Sofa opposite -
The Sleet - than May, no Thee -

Did the Harebell loose her girdle
To the lover Bee
Would the Bee the Harebell *hallow*
Much as formerly?

Did the "Paradise" - *persuaded* -
Yield her moat of pearl -
Would the Eden *be* an Eden,
Or the Earl - an *Earl?*

A Charm invests a face
Imperfectly beheld -
The Lady dare not lift her Vail
For fear it be dispelled -

But peers beyond her mesh -
And wishes - and denies -
Lest Interview - annul a want
That Image - satisfies -

The Rose did caper on her cheek -
Her Boddice rose and fell -
Her pretty speech - like drunken men -
Did stagger pitiful -

Her fingers fumbled at her work -
Her needle would not go -
What ailed so smart a little maid -
It puzzled me to know -

Till opposite - I spied a cheek
That bore *another* Rose -
Just opposite - another speech
That like the Drunkard goes -

A Vest that like her Boddice, danced -
To the immortal tune -
Till those two troubled - little Clocks
Ticked softly into one.

In lands I never saw - they say
Immortal Alps look down -
Whose Bonnets touch the firmament -
Whose sandals touch the town;

Meek at whose everlasting feet
A myriad Daisy play -
Which, Sir, are you, and which am *I* -
Opon an August day?

The Moon is distant from the Sea -
And yet, with Amber Hands -
She leads Him - docile as a Boy -
Along appointed Sands -

He never misses a Degree -
Obedient to Her eye -
He comes just so far - toward the Town -
Just so far - goes away -

Oh, Signor, Thine, the Amber Hand -
And mine - the distant Sea -
Obedient to the least command
Thine eye impose on me -

He put the Belt around my life -
I heard the Buckle snap -
And turned away, imperial,
My Lifetime folding up -
Deliberate, as a Duke would do
A Kingdom's Title Deed -
Henceforth - a Dedicated sort -
A Member of the Cloud -

Yet not too far to come at call -
And do the little Toils
That make the Circuit of the Rest -
And deal occasional smiles
To lives that stoop to notice mine -
And kindly ask it in -
Whose invitation, know you not
For Whom I must decline?

I held a Jewel in my fingers -
And went to sleep -
The day was warm, and winds were prosy -
I said "'Twill keep" -

I woke - and chid my honest fingers,
The Gem was gone -
And now, an Amethyst remembrance
Is all I own -

What if I say I shall not wait!
What if I burst the fleshly Gate -
And pass Escaped - to thee!

What if I file this mortal - off -
See where it hurt me - That's enough -
And wade in Liberty!

They cannot take me - any more!
Dungeons can call - and Guns implore -
Unmeaning - now - to me -

As laughter - was - an hour ago -
Or Laces - or a Travelling Show -
Or who died - yesterday!

Proud of my broken heart, since thou did'st break it,
Proud of the pain I did not feel till thee,

Proud of my night, since thou with moons dost slake it,
Not to partake thy passion, my humility.

Thou can'st not boast, like Jesus, drunken without companion
Was the strong cup of anguish brewed for the Nazarene

Thou can'st not pierce tradition with the peerless puncture,
See! I usurped thy crucifix to honor mine!

My Worthiness is all my Doubt -
His Merit - all my fear -
Contrasting which, my quality
Do lowlier - appear -

Lest I should insufficient prove
For His beloved Need -
The Chiefest Apprehension
Opon my thronging Mind -

'Tis true - that Deity to stoop
Inherently incline -
For nothing higher than Itself
Itself can rest opon -

So I - the Undivine Abode
Of His Elect Content -
Conform my Soul - as 'twere a Church,
Unto Her Sacrament -

Love - is anterior to Life -
Posterior - to Death -
Initial of Creation, and
The Exponent of Earth -

One Blessing had I than the rest
So larger to my Eyes
That I stopped guaging - satisfied -
For this enchanted size -

It was the limit of my Dream -
The focus of my Prayer -
A perfect - paralyzing Bliss -
Contented as Despair -

I knew no more of Want - or Cold -
Phantasms both become
For this new Value in the Soul -
Supremest Earthly Sum -

The Heaven below the Heaven above -
Obscured with ruddier Blue -
Life's Latitudes leant over - full -
The Judgment perished - too -

Why Bliss so scantily disburse -
Why Paradise defer -
Why Floods be served to Us - in Bowls -
I speculate no more -

When Roses cease to bloom, Sir,
And Violets are done -
When Bumblebees in solemn flight
Have passed beyond the Sun -
The hand that paused to gather
Opon this Summer's day
Will idle lie - in Auburn -
Then take my flowers - pray!

Summer for thee, grant I may be
When Summer days are flown!
Thy music still, when Whippowil
And Oriole - are done!

For thee to bloom, I'll skip the tomb
And row my blossoms o'er!
Pray gather me -
Anemone -
Thy flower - forevermore!

Split the Lark - and you'll find the Music -
Bulb after Bulb, in Silver rolled -
Scantily dealt to the Summer Morning
Saved for your Ear, when Lutes be old -

Loose the Flood - you shall find it patent -
Gush after Gush, reserved for you -
Scarlet Experiment! Sceptic Thomas!
Now, do you doubt that your Bird was true?

To lose thee - sweeter than to gain
All other hearts I knew.
'Tis true the drought is destitute,
But then, I had the dew!

The Caspian has it's realms of sand,
It's other realm of sea.
Without the sterile perquisite,
No Caspian could be.

Poor little Heart!
Did they forget thee?
Then dinna care! Then dinna care!

Proud little Heart!
Did they forsake thee?
Be debonnaire! Be debonnaire!

Frail little Heart!
I would not break thee -
Could'st credit *me?* Could'st credit me?

Gay little Heart -
Like Morning Glory!
Wind and Sun - wilt thee array!

There is a word
Which bears a sword
Can pierce an armed man -
It hurls it's barbed syllables
And is mute again -
But where it fell
The saved will tell
On patriotic day,
Some epauletted Brother
Gave his breath away.

Wherever runs the breathless sun -
Wherever roams the day,
There is it's noiseless onset -
There is it's victory!
Behold the keenest marksman!
The most accomplished shot!
Time's sublimest target
Is a soul "forgot"!

I've got an arrow here.
Loving the hand that sent it
I the dart revere.

Fell, they will say, in "skirmish"!
Vanquished, my soul will know
By but a simple arrow
Sped by an archer's bow.

He fumbles at your Soul
As Players at the Keys -
Before they drop full Music on -
He stuns you by Degrees -

Prepares your brittle nature
For the etherial Blow
By fainter Hammers - further heard -
Then nearer - Then so - slow -

Your Breath - has time to straighten -
Your Brain - to bubble cool -
Deals One - imperial Thunderbolt -
That scalps your naked soul -

When Winds hold Forests in their Paws -
The Universe - is still -

Heart! We will forget him!
You and I - tonight!
You may forget the warmth he gave -
I will forget the light!

When you have done, pray tell me
That I may straight begin!
Haste! lest while you're lagging
I remember him!

Father - I bring thee - not myself -
That were the little load -
I bring thee the imperial Heart
I had not strength to hold -

The Heart I cherished in my own
Till mine - too heavy grew -
Yet - strangest - heavier - since it went -
Is it too large for you?

We outgrow love, like other things
And put it in the Drawer -
Till it an Antique fashion shows -
Like Costumes Grandsires wore

Not with a Club, the Heart is broken
Nor with a Stone -
A Whip so small you could not see it
I've known

To lash the Magic Creature
Till it fell,
Yet that Whip's Name
Too noble then to tell.

Magnanimous as Bird
By Boy descried -
Singing unto the Stone
Of which it died -

Shame need not crouch
In such an Earth as Our's -
Shame - stand erect -
The Universe is your's.

My friend must be a Bird -
Because it flies!
Mortal, my friend must be -
Because it dies!
Barbs has it, like a Bee!
Ah, curious friend!
Thou puzzlest me!

He touched me, so I live to know
That such a day, permitted so,
I groped opon his breast -

It was a boundless place to me
And silenced, as the awful Sea
Puts minor streams to rest.

And now, I'm different from before,
As if I breathed superior air -
Or brushed a Royal Gown -
My feet, too, that had wandered so -
My Gypsy face - transfigured now -
To tenderer Renown -

Into this Port, if I might come,
Rebecca, to Jerusalem,
Would not so ravished turn -
Nor Persian, baffled at her shrine
Lift such a Crucifixal sign
To her imperial Sun.

Let me not mar that perfect Dream
By an Auroral stain
But so adjust my daily Night
That it will come again.

Not when we know, the Power accosts -
The Garment of Surprise
Was all our timid Mother wore
At Home - in Paradise.

I live with Him - I see His face -
I go no more away
For Visitor - or Sundown -
Death's single privacy

The Only One - forestalling Mine -
And that - by Right that He
Presents a Claim invisible -
No Wedlock - granted Me -

I live with Him - I hear His Voice -
I stand alive - Today -
To witness to the Certainty
Of Immortality -

Taught Me - by Time - the lower Way -
Conviction - every day -
That Life like This - is stopless -
Be Judgment - what it may -

I envy Seas, whereon He rides -
I envy Spokes of Wheels
Of Chariots, that Him convey -
I envy Crooked Hills

That gaze opon His journey -
How easy all can see
What is forbidden utterly
As Heaven - unto me!

I envy Nests of Sparrows -
That dot His distant Eaves;
The wealthy Fly, opon His Pane -
The happy - happy Leaves -

That just abroad His Window
Have Summer's leave to play -
The Ear Rings of Pizarro
Could not obtain for me -

I envy Light - that wakes Him -
And Bells - that boldly ring
To tell Him it is Noon, abroad -
Myself - be Noon to Him -

Yet interdict - my Blossom -
And abrogate - my Bee -
Lest Noon in everlasting night -
Drop Gabriel - and me -

Title divine, is mine.
The Wife without the Sign -
Acute Degree conferred on me -
Empress of Calvary -
Royal, all but the Crown -
Betrothed, without the Swoon
God gives us Women -
When You hold Garnet to Garnet -
Gold - to Gold -
Born - Bridalled - Shrouded -
In a Day -
Tri Victory -
"My Husband" - Women say
Stroking the Melody -
Is this the way -

I should not dare to leave my friend,
Because - because if he should die
While I was gone - and I - too late -
Should reach the Heart that wanted me -

If I should disappoint the eyes
That hunted - hunted so - to see -
And could not bear to shut until
They "noticed" me - they noticed me -

If I should stab the patient faith
So sure I'd come - so sure I'd come -
It listening - listening - went to sleep -
Telling my tardy name -

My Heart would wish it broke before -
Since breaking then - since breaking then -
Were useless as next morning's sun -
Where midnight frosts - had lain!

One Sister have I in the house -
And one a hedge away.
There's only one recorded -
But both belong to me.

One came the road that I came -
And wore my last year's gown -
The other, as a bird her nest
Builded our hearts among.

She did not sing as we did -
It was a different tune -
Herself to her a music
As Bumble bee of June.

Today is far from childhood,
But up and down the hills,
I held her hand the tighter -
Which shortened all the miles -

And still her hum
The years among,
Deceives the Butterfly;
And in her Eye
The Violets lie,
Mouldered this many May -

I spilt the dew,
But took the morn -
I chose this single star
From out the wide night's numbers -
Sue - forevermore!

Beauty crowds me till I die
Beauty mercy have on me
But if I expire today
Let it be in sight of thee -

The Luxury to apprehend
The Luxury 'twould be
To look at thee a single time
An Epicure of me
In whatsoever presence makes
Till for a further food
I scarcely recollect to starve
So first am I supplied.

The Luxury to meditate
The Luxury it was
To banquet on thy Countenance
A sumptuousness supplies
To plainer Days whose Table, far
As Certainty can see
Is laden with a single Crumb -
The Consciousness of thee -

Love reckons by itself - alone -
"As large as I" - relate the Sun
To One who never felt it blaze -
Itself is all the like it has -

Distance - is not the Realm of Fox
Nor by Relay of Bird
Abated - Distance is
Until thyself, Beloved.

How destitute is he
Whose Gold is firm
Who finds it every time
The small stale Sum
When Love with but a Pence
Will so display
As is a disrespect
To India

To love thee Year by Year -
May less appear
Than sacrifice, and cease -
However, dear,
Forever might be short, I thought to show -
And so I pieced it, with a flower, now.

He showed me Hights I never saw -
"Would'st Climb" - He said?
I said, "Not so" -
"With me -" He said - "With me"?

He showed me secrets - Morning's Nest -
The Rope the Nights were put across -
"And now, Would'st have me for a Guest"?
I could not find my "Yes" -

And then - He brake His Life - And lo,
A light for me, did solemn glow -
The larger, as my face withdrew -
And could I further "No"?

If I could tell how glad I was
I should not be so glad -
But when I cannot make the Force
Nor mould it into word
I know it is a sign
That new Dilemma be
From mathematics further off
Than from Eternity

The Sea said "Come" to the Brook -
The Brook said "Let me grow" -
The Sea said "then you will be a Sea -
I want a Brook - Come now"!

The Sea said "Go" to the Sea -
The Sea said "I am he
You cherished" - "Learned Waters -
Wisdom is stale - to Me" -

Her Grace is all she has -
And that, so least displays -
One Art to recognize, must be,
Another Art, to praise -

To see her is a Picture -
To hear her is a Tune -
To know her, a disparagement of every other
    Boon -
To know her not, Affliction -
To own her for a Friend
A warmth as near as if the Sun
Were shining in your Hand -

So set it's Sun in Thee
What Day be dark to me
What Distance far
So I the Ships may see
That touch how seldomly
Thy Shore?

Had this one Day not been,
Or could it cease to be
How smitten, how superfluous,
Were every other Day!

Lest Love should value less
What Loss would value more
Had it the stricken privilege,
It cherishes before.

That she forgot me was the least
I felt it second pain
That I was worthy to forget
Was most I thought upon

Faithful was all that I could boast
But Constancy became
To her, by her innominate
A something like a shame

The incidents of Love
Are more than it's Events -
Investment's best expositor
Is the minute Per Cents -

A little overflowing word
That any, hearing, had inferred
For Ardor or for Tears,
Though Generations pass away,
Traditions ripen and decay,
As eloquent appears -

Just so - Christ - raps -
He - does'nt weary -
First at the Knocker -
And then - at the Bell -
Then - on Divinest tiptoe standing -
Might he but spy the hiding soul!

When he - retires -
Chilled - or weary -
It will be ample time for me -
Patient - opon the steps - until then -
Heart - I am knocking low
At thee!

Safe Despair it is that raves -
Agony is frugal.
Puts itself severe away
For it's own perusal.

Garrisoned no Soul can be
In the Front of Trouble -
Love is one, not aggregate -
Nor is Dying double -

The Face we choose to miss -
Be it but for a Day
As absent as a Hundred Years,
When it has rode away -

Of so divine a Loss
We enter but the Gain,
Indemnity for Loneliness
That such a Bliss has been.

The healed Heart shows it's shallow scar
With confidential moan -
Not mended by Mortality
Are Fabrics truly torn -
To go it's convalescent way
So shameless is to see
More genuine were perfidy
Than such Fidelity -

To pile like Thunder to it's close
Then crumble grand away
While everything created hid
This - would be Poetry -

Or Love - the two coeval come -
We both and neither prove -
Experience either and consume -
For none see God and live -

I did not reach Thee
But my feet slip nearer every day
Three Rivers and a Hill to cross
One Desert and a Sea
I shall not count the journey one
When I am telling thee

Two deserts but the year is cold
So that will help the sand
One desert crossed -
The second one
Will feel as cool as land
Sahara is too little price
To pay for thy Right hand

The Sea comes last - Step merry feet
So short we have to go
To play together we are prone
But we must labor now
The last shall be the lightest load
That we have had to draw

The Sun goes crooked -
That is Night
Before he makes the bend
We must have passed the Middle Sea
Almost we wish the End
Were further off
Too great it seems
So near the Whole to stand

We step like Plush
We stand like snow
The waters murmur new
Three rivers and the Hill are passed
Two deserts and the Sea!
Now Death usurps my Premium
And gets the look at Thee -

Love - is that later Thing than Death -
More previous - than Life -
Confirms it at it's entrance - And
Usurps it - of itself -

Tastes Death - the first - to hand the sting
The Second - to it's friend -
Disarms the little interval -
Deposits Him with God -

Then hovers - an inferior Guard -
Lest this Beloved Charge
Need - once in an Eternity -
A smaller than the Large -

To Susan Gilbert (Dickinson), April 5, 1852

Monday morning-
Will you be kind to me, Susie? I am naughty and cross, this morning, and nobody loves me here; nor would *you* love me, if you should see me frown, and hear how loud the door bangs whenever I go through; and yet it is'nt anger-I dont believe it is, for when nobody sees, I brush away big tears with the corner of my apron, and then go working on-bitter tears, Susie, so hot that they burn cheeks, and almost schorch my eyeballs, but you have wept such, and you know they are less of anger than *sorrow.*

And I do love to run fast, and hide away from them all; here in dear Susie's bosom, I know is love and rest, and I never would go away, did not the big world call me, and beat me for not working.

Little *Emerald Mack* is washing, I can hear the warm suds, splash, I just gave her my pocket handkerchief-so I cannot cry any more. And Vinnie sweeps-sweeps, opon the chamber stairs; and Mother is hurrying round with her hair in a silk pocket handkerchief, on account of dust. Oh Susie, it is dismal, sad and drear eno', and the sun dont shine, and the clouds look cold and gray, and the wind dont blow, but it *pipes* the shrill-est roundelay, and the birds dont sing, but twitter-and there's nobody to smile! Do I paint it *natural*-Susie, so you think how it looks? Yet dont you care-for it wont last so always, and we love you just as well, and think of you just as dearly, as if it were not so. Your precious letter, Susie, it sits here now, and smiles so kindly at me, and gives me such sweet thoughts of the dear writer. When you come home, darling, I shant have your letters, shall I, but I shall have *yourself,* which is more-Oh more, and better, than I can even think! I sit here with my little whip, cracking the time away, till not an hour is left of it-then you are here! And *Joy* is here –joy now and forevermore!

Tis only a few days, Susie, it will soon go away, yet I say, go now, this very, very moment, for I need her, I must have her, Oh give her to me!

Mattie is dear and true, I love her very dearly, and Emily Fowler, too, is very dear to me–and Tempe, and Abby, and Eme', I am sure I love them all–and I hope they love me, but, Susie, there's a great corner still; I fill it with that is gone, I hover round and round it, and call it darling names, and bid it speak to me, and ask it if it's Susie, and it answers, Nay, Ladie, Susie is stolen away!

Do I repine, is it all murmuring, or am I sad and lone, and cannot, cannot help it? Sometimes when I do feel so, I think it may be wrong, and that God will punish me by taking you away; for he is very kind to let me write to you, and to give me your sweet letters, but my heart wants *more*.

Have you ever thought of it Susie, and yet I know you have, how much these hearts claim; why I dont believe in the whole, wide world, are such hard little creditors, such real little *misers,* as you and I carry with us, in our bosoms every day. I cant help thinking sometimes, when I hear about the ungenerous, Heart, keep very still–or someone will find you out!

I am going out on the doorstep, to get you some new-green grass–I shall pick it down in the corner, where you and I used to sit, and have long fancies. And perhaps the dear little grasses were growing all the while–and perhaps they heard what we said, but they cant *tell!* I have come in now, dear Susie, and here is what I found–not quite so glad and green as when we used to sit there, but a sad and pensive grassie–mourning o'er hopes. No doubt some spruce, young *Plantain leaf* won its young heart away, and then proved false–and dont you wish none proved so, but little Plantains?

I do think it's wonderful, Susie, that our hearts dont break, *every day,* when I think of all the whiskers, and all the gallant men, but I guess I'm made with nothing but a hard heart of stone, for it dont break any, and dear Susie, if mine is stony, your's is stone, opon stone, for you never yield *any*, where I seem quite beflown. Are we going to *ossify* always, say, Susie, how will it be? When I see the Popes and the Polloks, and the John-Milton Browns, I think we are *liable*, but I dont know! I am glad there's a big *future* waiting for me and you. You would love to know what I read–I hardly know what to tell you, my cata logue is so small.

I have just read three little books, not great, not thrilling, but sweet and true. "The Light in the Valley," "Only," and a " House upon a Rock." I know you would love them all, yet they dont *bewitch* me any. There are no walks in the wood–no low and earnest voices, no moonlight, nor stolen love, but pure little lives, loving God, and their parents, and obeying the laws of the land; yet read, if you meet them, Susie, for they will do one good.

I have the promise of "Alton Lock"–a certain book, called "Olive," and the "Head of a Family," which was what Mattie named to you. Vinnie and I had "Bleak House" sent to us the other day–it is like him who wrote it–that is all I can say. Dear Susie, you were so happy when you wrote to me last–I am so glad, and you will be happy *now* for *all* my sadness, *wont* you? I cant forgive me ever, if I have made you sad, or dimmed your eye for me. I write from the Land of Violets, and from the Land of Spring, and it would ill become me to carry you nought but sorrows. I remember you, Susie, *always*–I keep you ever here, and when *you* are gone, then I'm gone–and we're 'neath one willow tree. I can only thank "the Father" for giving me such as you, I can only pray unceasingly, that he will bless my Loved One, and bring her back to me, to "go no more out forever." ["] Herein is Love." But *that* was Heaven–*this* is but *Earth,* yet Earth so *like* to heaven, that I would hesitate, should the true one call away. Dear Susie–adieu! Emilie–

The scope of Emily Dickinson's poetry is the entire universe, circumferenced by a mind that finds the utmost beauty in a tiny spider, and then, in the space of two words, moves from that beauty to the cosmos. Dickinson ushers in a new mode of perception, where we get close to *feeling* our understanding of things. Dickinson's circumstances were deliberately tightly drawn around her when she decided, at a certain point in life, not to venture out of her father's house in Amherst, Massachusetts, where she had grown up. Her self-imposed exile—a radical and outrageous rebellion against the expectations that imprisoned women of her time—liberated her to a large extent from the obligations of society. Her niece, who also put together the volumes of poetry from which this selection is gathered, reported that her aunt responded sharply to a suggestion that time must pass slowly for her in her lonely room: "Time, why, Time was all I wanted!"

She used her hard-won time to produce nearly 1,800 poems on a wide range of topics. Only eleven were published in her lifetime; ten of those anonymously, and probably submitted by friends without Dickinson's knowledge They have in common her idiosyncratic use of grammar, her indifference to conventional punctuation, and her incredibly powerful capacity to transfigure the religious and literary idioms available during her time—including William Shakespeare, Elizabeth Barrett Browning, Robert Browning, the Brontës, and the transcendentalists. The poet Susan Howe, in an inspired book on Dickinson that obliterates the stereotype of the recluse spinster in the attic, remarks that poetry creates "[c]onnections between unconnected things [in] unreal reality." Connecting unconnected things through the power of naming and language, and in a reality that, once named in this poetic way, seems unreal, removed from the familiarity of regular space and time: this is also what we call love. Not as a feeling that passes, but as a condition in which a connection is possible that had previously not been there. The insight that Dickinson creates, or finds ("Connections between unconnected things"), allows us to read much of her poetry as a poetry of love. "Oh the Earth was *made* for lovers," Dickinson writes in an 1850 valentine, which was an immensely popular form in her days. For love is that unnamed thing that creates connection between unconnected things. But love should not be mistaken—nothing in Dickinson's poetry should ever be mistaken as definitively named—as connection itself, but as the *possibility* of connection. For love, in poetry and in life, where we step "from plank to plank" (where Dickinson, with her transcendental humor, also hears "blank"), must be expressed to be manifest.

For Dickinson, love becomes real only when imagined *and* expressed, not simply *felt*. Her poetry is devoted to examining our power of imagining and expressing the world as it is given to us and as it arises in our minds. The link between these two— outer world, inner reality—is what the poems constitute but do not name. The greatest minds of Dickinson's time, including Ralph Waldo Emerson (who stayed at the Dickinson home when he visited Amherst College) and Walt Whitman (whose *Leaves of Grass* was self-published in 1850), thought God, or Abraham Lincoln's "unfinished work," or poetry, or Whitman's "America" supplied this link. Dickinson, as Harold Bloom points out, deliberately unnames all these possibilities. She does so by way of striking paradox, but also by undercutting her own metaphors in sly, sometimes quite funny, and often startling, ways: "To make a prairie it takes a clover and one bee, / One clover, and a bee. / And revery. / The revery alone will do, / If bees are few." The poem starts as a recipe for *worlding* reality, then takes away the resulting image, drops the clover entirely, and ends with a joke: no bee is necessary. The conditions are named, then instantly discarded. The last line turns the poem's lofty premise into something like an afterthought. We could see the prairie with the clover and the bee, but imagination, here called "revery," is the only essential ingredient. Through such acts of doubling back on a metaphor, foiling our expectations for a phrase, playing with homonyms (bee and "be"), and inverting the order of what is great and what is small, Dickinson cracks open the confines of our thinking.

The poems in this book give voice to love as the uncanny force that creates connections between unconnected things. Dickinson herself experienced great love in her life. There were a few men, scholars believe; and we know, from some surviving letters, that the woman who married Dickinson's brother, Susan Gilbert, filled the young Dickinson's heart with an exuberance still palpable today: "[C]ome with me this morning to the church within our hearts, where the bells are always ringing, and the preacher whose name is Love—shall intercede there for us!" Through poetry Dickinson both performs and *examines* love in all its guises—love found, love lived, love lost—as deepening experience, which we can taste with tingling immediacy one and a half centuries later: "To lose thee, sweeter than to gain / All other hearts I knew. / 'T is true the drought is destitute, / But then I had the dew!"

In Dickinson the entirety of experience—joy and pain, possession and loss, solitariness and sociality—deepens rather than diminishes life. This persistent revelation turns Dickinson's verses (written on scraps of papers, envelopes, and other unusual surfaces) into experiences akin to epiphanies—in the sense that the readers have to experience them, unfold them, and, possibly, be enveloped by them. Most readers will not be fortunate to handle Dickinson's papers held in archives from Amherst to Washington, D.C.; they will not have the sensory experience of unfolding, holding, and feeling a Dickinson poem, light as a feather, feathered as a nest, nesting in one's palm, taking off with a breeze. Instead, they will read these poems (possibly through some of the stunning electronic archives of Dickinson's writings created by Ellen Louise Hart, Martha Nell Smith, and others at the University of Virginia and elsewhere) as messages from an exceptionally sharp mind, eager to communicate itself. The essence of Dickinson's poetry is her astounding capacity to use language as if she is directly transcribing her thoughts in their formation and motion, rather than as the finished products of her mind.

Dickinson's poems teach us to love: to approach another gently, yet filled with strong desire to possess them, and then to discover that *never* knowing someone fully—not completely understanding another—gives rise to more desire, more affection, more love. What makes her poetry so utterly unique, I think, is how she communicates with such gripping immediacy this quest to know and follow the workings and hesitations of her mind and heart. Introspection all too often turns lifeless because we cannot simultaneously feel and observe our feelings. With her extremely carefully selected words, taken from scripture, botany, anatomy, geography, literature, and other realms of life and study, Dickinson, poet not philosopher, makes the act of reflection come alive.

Dickinson sent poems and some very direct letters to Thomas Wentworth Higginson, an iconoclast, ardent abolitionist, Unitarian minister, and soldier who had published advice for aspiring writers just before joining the Union Army in the Civil War. Dickinson sought his professional guidance because, she noted, "The Mind is so near itself—it cannot see, distinctly." Her correspondence with Higginson evolved into a close lifelong friendship. Emily Dickinson wanted to be read but did not court fame; she carefully preserved for posterity nearly all 1,775 of her poems, stitched into small paper packets, in a trunk discovered only after her death in 1886. The biographer Brenda Wineapple explains how Dickinson shunned the "admiring Bog" of fame and yet, deeply convinced of her achievement, entrusted many poems to Higginson, a public figure who would ultimately publish most of her work. If this stance seems contradictory, it opens up a central concern as urgent today as in Dickinson's time: how to think for oneself in a world where one is pressured to publicize one's thoughts often before they are fully formed. Her sister Lavinia, who had been instrumental in keeping Emily's life free from many of the constraints most women faced during her time, turned them over to Higginson and Mabel Loomis Todd, who had a long affair with Emily's brother Austin. Higginson and Todd edited the material and began publishing it in 1890, together with some of Dickinson's letters; and later Austin's daughter, Martha Dickinson Bianchi (together with Alfred Leete Hampson), published several volumes. Publication of her work soon established Dickinson's reputation as one of America's greatest poets and one of the most original poets of all time, as affirmed by many superb scholars too numerous to list here. There are ongoing debates about editorial decisions of what constitutes a poem and what qualifies "only" as a letter, about how to classify a few words jotted on a scrap of paper or enfolded in the prose of letters, and how best to reproduce the marks Dickinson put in her poems, and whether to adapt idiosyncratic spellings to modern usage.

EMILY DICKINSON

Emily Dickinson was born in Amherst, Massachusetts, on December 10th, 1830, to the lawyer Edward and the home-maker Emily Norcross Dickinson. She grew up mostly in the family homestead in Amherst, which the family sold and later re-leased and finally bought back, in 1855, with two other siblings, older brother Austin and younger sister Lavinia, both of whom remained close to her throughout her life. She was well educated for a woman of that time, attending Amherst Academy for about seven years before enrolling at Mount Holyoke Female Seminary, now Mount Holyoke College, for a year in 1847. An avid student and reader, Dickinson took an interest in many subjects and participated in Amherst social life. She had several close female and male friends, including at least one confirmed suitor who proposed marriage.

In her early twenties, Dickinson started to write more seriously, though not with an eye to publication. She confided in her brother and friends that she was composing verses, some of which she included in her letters. She also decided to cease attending church, preferring instead to seek an experience of transcendence in nature, rather than through organized religion.

In 1856, her brother Austin married Dickinson's intimate friend, Susan Gilbert. Emily and Susan had exchanged a series of intimate letters that lead many scholars to believe that their relationship was more than just a friendship. The newlyweds built a house next door to the Dickinson family home, from where Emily communicated with great frequency with Susan, sometimes through letters and other missives deposited in the mailbox a few feet from Dickinson's and Susan's respective homes. We have excerpted one such letter written in 1852.

Between 1858 and 1865, Dickinson wrote hundreds of poems, ranging in subject matter from life, death, God, travels, love, and nature but all characterized by brief, sometimes staccato sentences, little or no formal punctuation, and creative verbal arrangements that produce startling effects via deceptively simple rhyming and patterns. During this period, she sent poems to friends and others, although she did not consent to having her poems published with her name.

In 1862, Dickinson contacted Thomas Higginson, an abolitionist, Unitarian Minister, soldier, and women's rights advocate who had written articles for the *Atlantic Monthly* magazine to inquire whether the poems she enclosed were "alive," but enigmatically did not sign them and instead enclosed a small separate envelope, with a card bearing her name. Higginson and Dickinson maintained a correspondence until her death, punctuated by rare personal visits, in 1870.

During the 1860s Dickinson increasingly withdrew from routine social interactions, preferring time in her room or gardening outside or in her interior conservatory to speaking with visitors to the house. Her sister Lavinia took on many of the duties Dickinson was expected to perform for the household.

Plagued by eye problems in the 1860s, Dickinson confronted a series of deaths when she was in her forties. Her father died in 1874, her mother suffered a stroke in 1875, her nephew did at age eight in 1883, her suitor Otis Lord died in 1884, and her friend Helen Hunt Jackson died in 1885. After a period of poor health, she Emily Dickinson died in 1886, and is buried at what is today known as the West Cemetery in Amherst, Massachusetts.

Index of First Lines